BOOKER T. WASHINGTON
AFRICAN-AMERICAN LEADER

Famous
African Americans

**Patricia and
Fredrick McKissack**

Enslow Elementary
an imprint of

Enslow Publishers, Inc.

40 Industrial Road
Box 398
Berkeley Heights, NJ 07922
USA

http://www.enslow.com

E

For Estelle and Mike Smith, Happy Memories

Enslow Elementary, an imprint of Enslow Publishers, Inc.

Enslow Elementary® is a registered trademark of Enslow Publishers, Inc.

Revised edition of *Booker T. Washington: Leader and Educator* © 1992

Library of Congress Cataloging-in-Publication Data

McKissack, Pat, 1944-
  Booker T. Washington : African-American leader / Patricia and Fredrick McKissack.
    p. cm. — (Famous African Americans)
  Includes bibliographical references and index.
  Summary: "A simple biography for early readers about Booker T. Washington's life"—Provided by publisher.
  ISBN 978-0-7660-4100-4
  1. Washington, Booker T., 1856–1915—Juvenile literature.
  2. African Americans—Biography—Juvenile literature.
  3. Educators—United States—Biography—Juvenile literature.
  4. Tuskegee Institute—Juvenile literature. I. McKissack, Fredrick.
  II. Title.
  E185.97.W4M33 2013
  370.92—dc23

[B]
                              2012011300

Future editions
Paperback ISBN 978-1-4644-0194-7
ePUB ISBN 978-1-4645-1107-3
PDF ISBN 978-1-4646-1107-0

Printed in the United States of America

082012 Lake Book Manufacturing, Inc., Melrose Park, IL

10 9 8 7 6 5 4 3 2 1

To Our Readers: We have done our best to make sure all Internet Addresses in this book were active and appropriate when we went to press. However, the author and the publisher have no control over and assume no liability for the material available on those Internet sites or on other Web sites they may link to. Any comments or suggestions can be sent by e-mail to comments@enslow.com or to the address on the back cover.

Every effort has been made to locate all copyright holders of material used in this book. If any errors or omissions have occurred, corrections will be made in future editions of this book.

♻ Enslow Publishers, Inc., is committed to printing our books on recycled paper. The paper in every book contains 10% to 30% post-consumer waste (PCW). The cover board on the outside of each book contains 100% PCW. Our goal is to do our part to help young people and the environment too!

Photo Credits: Library of Congress, pp. 1, 3, 4, 7 (both), 10 (both), 14, 20.

Illustration Credits: Michael Bryant, pp. 8, 13, 16.

Cover Credits: Library of Congress

Words in bold type are are explained in Words to Know on page 22.

Series Consultant:
Russell Adams, PhD
Emeritus Professor
Afro-American Studies
Howard University

CONTENTS

Booker T. Washington was born a slave, but he became the most powerful black leader of his time.

CHAPTER 1

FROM SLAVERY TO FREEDOM

Booker Taliaferro Washington never knew his birthday. He was born a **slave**, and the dates of slave births were not always written down. It is believed he was born sometime in 1856.

Booker and his family lived on a large Virginia **plantation**. His mother's name was Jane, and his stepfather was Washington Ferguson. Their one-room shack had a dirt floor. The door didn't shut well. The windows had no glass. There were cracks in the walls.

Booker didn't even have a bed. He slept on the floor next to his brother John and his sister Amanda. A fireplace warmed the cabin. But it was always too hot or too cold in their home.

When Booker was only five years old, his master put him to work. Booker fanned flies away from his master's table at mealtimes.

When he got older, he was given a new job. Every week he went to the mill with a load of corn. The corn was ground into meal there.

One day Booker passed by a school. He wanted to go inside. But slave children could not go to school. It was against the law!

In 1861, the **Civil War** began. Northern and Southern states were at war with each other.

Lots of people wanted to end slavery. In 1863, **President** Abraham Lincoln freed all slaves in the South. But some slaves didn't know that they were free until the war ended in 1865.

Northern soldiers came to the plantation where Booker and his family lived. The soldiers told them they were free. There was a lot of singing and shouting. Freedom had come at last!

Booker was born in a small cabin on a plantation in Virginia. This cabin was built to look like the original one.

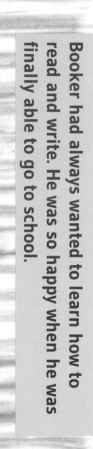

Booker had always wanted to learn how to read and write. He was so happy when he was finally able to go to school.

CHAPTER 2

FROM MALDEN TO HAMPTON

Booker and his family were free. But life was not much better for them. They could not read or write. They had no money, no jobs, and no home. How would they live? What could they do?

Booker's stepfather moved to Malden, West Virginia, and sent for his family. He found a job at a **salt furnace.** At the furnace, salt was boiled out of the water that came up from under the ground. Booker and his brother shoveled the salt into barrels.

Soon a school opened for black children in Malden. Booker finally got a chance to go to school.

The teacher asked him his name. He gave his first name, "Booker." The teacher wanted to know his last name. Booker did not know what to say. He had never had a last name. He thought about it. Then he told the teacher, "My name is Booker Washington."

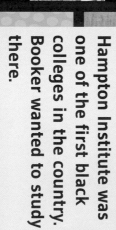

Hampton Institute was one of the first black colleges in the country. Booker wanted to study there.

Booker had to work in the coal mines, so he didn't go to school very often. But he read everything he could.

General Lewis Ruffner owned the salt furnace and coal mines in Malden. He hired Booker to do housework for his wife. Viola Ruffner was fussy and hard to please. She wanted everything to be spotless. Booker did his best to please her.

Viola Ruffner liked Booker. So she let him read her books. She talked to him a lot about going to school.

Booker heard about a school in Hampton, Virginia. He wanted to go there. He worked even harder and saved his money. In the fall of 1872, Booker had enough money. He left Malden to go to Hampton **Institute**. The school was five hundred miles away. Booker walked in the rain. He slept on the ground. He hopped trains and begged for rides on the backs of wagons. It was a long, hard trip. But he would not turn back.

11

CHAPTER 3

FROM HAMPTON TO TUSKEGEE

• •

Booker finally reached Hampton Institute. He was tired and dirty from traveling. He did not look like a student. Mary F. Mackie, the head teacher, told Booker there were no more openings. But then she told him to sweep a classroom floor. "Take the broom and sweep it," she said. She left Booker to do the job.

Viola Ruffner had taught Booker how to clean a room. He swept the classroom floor three times. Then he dusted it four times.

Mary Mackie came back later. She looked in the classroom and smiled. Then she decided to let him into the school. "I guess we will try you as a student," she said. Miss Mackie also hired Booker to be the **janitor**. And that is how he worked his way through school.

Booker showed Miss Mackie that he was a hard worker. She told him he could be a student at the school.

Booker loved learning.
He became a teacher
at Tuskegee Institute.

General Samuel C. Armstrong was the **principal** of Hampton. Most of the students who came to Hampton had been slaves. General Armstrong believed that learning a skill like bricklaying or carpentry was the best way for African Americans to better themselves. Booker believed this, too.

Booker **graduated** from the Hampton Institute in 1875. He taught for a while in Malden and he studied for a year at a school in Washington, D.C. In 1879, General Armstrong asked Booker to come back to Hampton.

There, Booker helped teach the Native American students. He did the job very well. He was put in charge of the night school for adults by the end of the next year.

General Armstrong got a letter from a group of people in Tuskegee, Alabama. They needed a principal to help start a school. General Armstrong gave them Booker T. Washington's name. They offered Booker the job.

The students and teachers of Tuskegee worked together to get their school ready.

CHAPTER 4

THE TUSKEGEE DREAM

Booker reached Tuskegee in June 1881. He had lots of students. But he did not have a place to hold classes. He did not have any school supplies either.

That didn't stop Booker. He held his first class in a Tuskegee church on July 4, 1881. Thirty students came to the class. Booker was the only teacher.

Six weeks passed. The school was still open. Booker hired Olivia Davidson to be his first teacher. She is often called the cofounder of Tuskegee. She was in charge of all the women students. Everyone called her Miss D.

Three months after the school opened, some friends helped Booker buy an old farm. Booker, Miss D., and their students scrubbed and cleaned the buildings. Many people gave gifts for the school. Sometimes they gave money. Sometimes they gave food. Booker was happy to get any help he could.

17

That is how Booker kept Tuskegee Institute open for a year. His work at Tuskegee became well known. Many people helped to make the Tuskegee dream come true. They gave their time and money.

Booker wanted Tuskegee to be a fine **trade school** just like Hampton Institute. And it was. His students were learning how to lay brick, cut stone, and make a suit. He liked to show visitors around. Most of the buildings were built by Tuskegee students and teachers. They also grew their own food at the Tuskegee farm.

Booker was married three times. His first wife was his childhood friend Fannie Smith. They had one daughter, Portia. Later, Fannie had a terrible fall. She died on May 4, 1884.

Booker married Miss D. a year later. They had two sons, Booker Jr. and Ernest Davidson. Olivia worked beside her husband until she died on May 9, 1889.

Margaret Murray came to Tuskegee as a teacher. A year later, she was named the new principal for women students. In time she became Booker's wife. They were married in 1892. He was 36 years old and she was 31.

CHAPTER 5

FROM POVERTY TO FAME

In the 1890s, African Americans were losing their right to vote. Unfair laws were being passed that took away many of their civil rights. **Frederick Douglass**, the most well-known black leader, died in 1895. People were wondering who would be the new black leader.

Booker gave a very important speech at the **Atlanta Cotton Exposition** on September 18, 1895. He said in his speech that the races could be as "separate as the fingers" on the hand in all social things. But when the country was in need (such as during war), the races could work together as one, like the fist.

Afterward, Booker T. Washington became the most powerful black leader of that time.

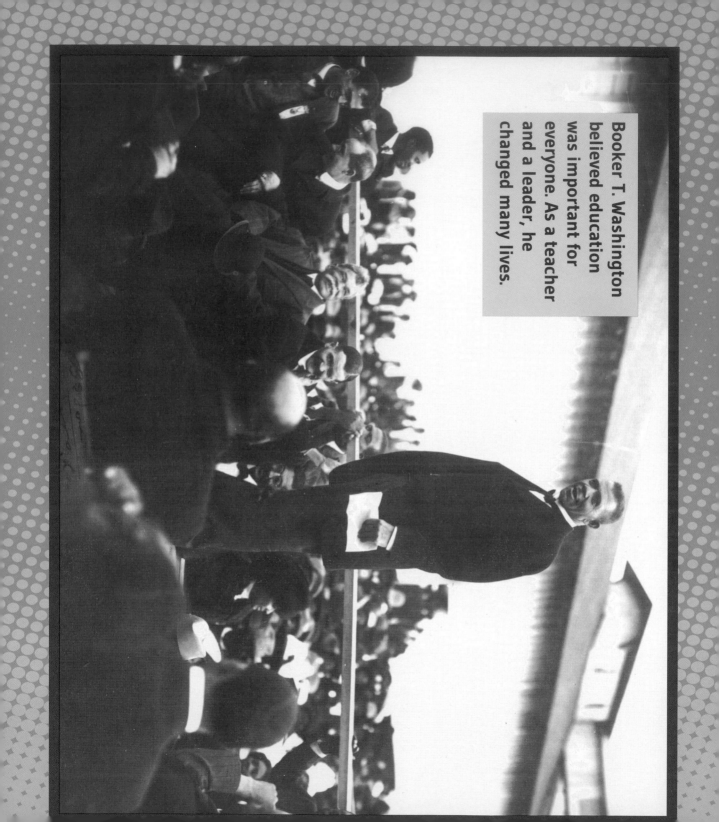

Booker T. Washington believed education was important for everyone. As a teacher and a leader, he changed many lives.

Many white people liked what Booker said. He was the leader they wanted. African Americans were divided. Some agreed with him. Others did not like his ideas. Many African Americans did not like white people telling them who their leaders should be.

Booker became a very powerful man. He talked with presidents and rich **businessmen**. In 1900, he started the **National Negro Business League**. The group tried to get more black businesses started.

Booker T. Washington was a very busy man, but he took time to write a book about his life. He called it *Up From Slavery*. He also enjoyed taking care of his garden, fishing, riding his horse, and telling visitors about the Tuskegee dream.

During a trip to New York, Booker became sick. Margaret went to bring him home. Booker T. Washington died a few hours after he got home to Alabama on November 14, 1915.

WORDS TO KNOW

Atlanta Cotton Exposition—A large business and industry fair held in 1895. The South wanted to show how much progress it had made since the Civil War.

businessman—A person who earns money by selling a product or service.

civil war—A war fought within a country. The United States Civil War (1861–1865) was fought between northern and southern states.

Frederick Douglass—A black leader who worked to end slavery.

graduate—To finish a course of study at a school.

institute—A place of learning; a school.

janitor—A person who keeps a building clean.

National Negro Business League—A group that was created to help African Americans open more businesses.

plantation—A large farm. When Booker was born, many slaves worked in the fields at plantations.

president—The head of a country or a group.

principal—The head of a school.

salt furnace—A place where salt was boiled out of water brought up from underground.

slave—A person who is owned by another person and forced to work for no pay.

trade school—A school where students learn how to be skilled craftsmen, such as carpenters, bricklayers, tailors, and printers.

Learn More

Books

Brimner, Larry Dane. *Booker T. Washington: Getting Into the Schoolhouse.* Tarrytown, N.Y.: Marshall Cavendish, 2008.

Slade, Suzanne. *Booker T. Washington: Teacher, Speaker, and Leader.* Minneapolis : Picture Window Books, 2008.

Taylor-Butler, Christine. *Booker T. Washington.* New York: Children's Press, 2007.

Web Sites

Booker T. Washington

<http://gardenofpraise.com/ibdbookr.htm>

Legends of Tuskegee

<http://www.nps.gov/history/museum/exhibits/tuskegee/>

INDEX